The Relationship Code

The Relationship Code

10 Proven Strategies to
Avoid Every Bad Relationship
and Find Only Good Ones

Heron Free, M.Ed.

TheRelationshipCode.com

This book is dedicated to anyone
who has had their heart broken
and is looking to understand why.

The Relationship Code: 10 Proven Strategies to Avoid
Every Bad Relationship and Find Only Good Ones

Smart Minds Publishing
Calgary, Alberta, Canada
www.smartminds.ca

ISBN: 978-0-9950083-0-4

Printed in the United States of America

Table of Contents

Foreword

In *The Relationship Code*, master psychologist and relationship expert Heron Free, M.Ed., R.Psych., challenges you to think differently about your relationships and why they fail.

All of us start with the intention of wanting to be in a great relationship, but somewhere along the way something goes wrong.

It can be confusing and lead to a lot of heartbreak.

In this book, Heron offers up the intuitive and practical wisdom that he's shared with thousands of clients in his private practice over the last sixteen years.

Heron answers the age-old question about relationships: "Why do you choose the wrong person?"

This book will also teach you how to heal from past heartbreaks, break long-standing poor relationships patterns, and choose the right person in the future.

Reading Heron's book feels more as though you're having a trusted conversation with your therapist than anything else. Heron's deep insights into relationships and human behavior will change the way you see relationships for years to come.

If you're looking to gain deeper insight into the choices you are making in relationships and how to avoid the duds and find a truly great partner, I highly recommend this book.

Raymond Aaron
NY Times Best-Selling Author

Introduction

When I was thirty-four, I met a girl on an online dating site. She seemed interesting enough—a cute yoga instructor with similar interests. We chatted back and forth through email, but she didn't seem particularly interested in meeting; online dating can be pretty hit or miss. The next day, however, when I was looking to go to my next yoga class, I discovered that she was my instructor.

So I went to her class. After that, I wasn't particularly interested in reconnecting, as I didn't feel a spark. What happened afterward is the reason I wrote this book.

By chance, this woman had worked at the clinic where I was currently employed. And she knew my cousin who also worked there. So I called him, and our exchange went like this:

"Hey, guess who I met?" and then I told him her name.

"What? You have to stay away from her," he told me. I was shocked.

And—no exaggeration—someone else in the office

who heard her name grabbed the phone and yelled into it.

"You need to stay away from that woman. She treats her boyfriends terribly. She will make you run her errands and take care of her little dog."

Something in my mind clicked. I could feel it like a key turning in a lock. Now she sounded interesting.

And we started dating.

Guess what happened? She didn't treat me very well. Eventually, I got so lost in the relationship that I told her I wanted to marry her. Two days after that, she broke up with me. Why do we choose people who are wrong for us—even when our friends and family are telling us to stay away?

The goal of this book is to help you identify the unconscious choices that get you into bad relationships. You will also be provided with new strategies to help you attract healthier, happier ones.

The eventual outcome is a happier you and the ability to create the relationships you have always wanted.

CHAPTER 1

How Not to Be Left Standing by the Side of the Road

Strategy #1
Avoid Dramatic Relationships

There are many strategies you can follow when trying to avoid a bad relationship, but the most important is strategy number 1: Avoid Drama.

During the best of times, drama is a nuisance. During the worst of times, it is a full-blown catastrophe, with your clothes ending up in the front yard and the police getting involved. Drama causes loss of faith in ourselves, others, and the world. Dramatic relationships can also be very costly, such as a divorce that costs $100,000 or a couple spending $15,000 in legal fees fighting over who gets the family dog (true story; in the end, the husband gave it to his wife).

But we humans have a problem. We like drama. Drama is interesting. It can energize a bland, ho-hum day. It makes us feel more important, makes us feel alive.

Drama is our guilty pleasure. It's an addiction, really. It's the story in our own mind that creates excitement and makes life more interesting.

And while it's okay to watch the occasional reality show for fun, it's quite another matter to choose romantic relationships because they have drama. Some situations can be obvious, like living with an alcoholic, and others can be subtle, such as having a partner who never communicates his or her feelings.

But if drama is so bad for us, why are we attracted to it? To understand that, we must understand how it is created.

The Physiology of Drama

Drama is created when a story you have in your mind is combined with your physiological response to that story—essentially, how the story makes you feel emotionally.

Let's say you're a woman, and you meet a dashing man somewhere randomly. He shows up at your work the next day and brings you flowers. Great story! A physiological response occurs in you. Emotions, thoughts, and chemicals are released in your body. If you like how he made you feel, you will want to see him again. Of course, if you're horrified by him showing up at your place of work (not a great story), you will have a very different physiological interpretation of the event, and you'll be completely turned off.

Your physiological response bonds you to the story of you and him. If it's of high intensity, you'll remember it more; if it's of low intensity, you'll remember it less. It doesn't matter whether the experience is good or bad—the more intense, the more memorable.

These physiological responses are powerful, and when combined with the right story (the more Cinderella-like the better), they unconsciously drive human behavior and create strong attachments. In fact, most choices initially made when selecting a mate are not based on logic but rather on a physiological response and its complementary story line. You don't even really see the person. This person could be a psychopath or be married (or both), but you don't know that in the moment. All you know is that he made you feel good and there's a good storyline in there somewhere. Logic takes a backseat.

We are often unconsciously driven by our emotions alone when choosing mates, even when logic or a friend warns you that what you're doing is a bad idea. This is how you draw a lot of drama into your life and end up in a bad relationship that is difficult to untangle yourself from.

And that's why drama is very dangerous if you want

to find a really good person. People like to complete the story they have in their head so much that they miss seeing the person they are actually dating.

I often recommend to my clients, if they meet someone they are really excited about, that they take some time to sit by themselves after the date and contemplate whether this person is an ideal fit for them and to look beyond the story. Asking this question works wonders because they are not immersed in the situation and being affected by the great chemistry and thoughts of what could be. They can relax and see things more clearly. They then have the time to properly reflect and develop a plan of action to ensure that they are getting their needs met.

It also gives my clients the opportunity to focus back on their own life. Doing this helps them remember that they are powerful and unique individuals who are already doing the things that make them happy.

And that a new relationship is simply an enhancement to the life they already have.

Why We Remember the Jerks More Than the Nice People

So why is it that some people stick in our mind and we can't stop thinking about them?

Sometimes it seems we have little control over who

we are thinking about. It happens automatically. How does the mind decide what to obsess about and what to discard?

One of the ways the mind decides is by gauging the emotional intensity of an experience. The more emotionally intense an event, the more the mind assumes it is also meaningful. These intense events are then stored in long-term memory.

Have you ever been having a great time with everyone, and then one person insults you? Why is it that's the only person you think about for the whole night afterward? Maybe you even play out a scenario in your mind of what you will say to that person if you ever see him or her again. You never do, of course, but that doesn't stop your mind from thinking about how you might confront the person someday.

If an experience is emotionally intense or incongruent with how you are experiencing the world, it is a threat to your emotional (or mental) equilibrium and the peace and ease you were experiencing before the event occurred.

To restore equilibrium, the mind then tries to make sense of what happened—in this case, someone who was rude to you at a party. First, you might blame yourself and wonder: "Did I do something wrong to offend this person?" Or you might blame them instead: "That person was a real jerk." Or you might just generalize about the world: "People will always try to knock you down when they can."

But none of the three scenarios is likely to help, because in all of the situations, you are still thinking more, not less. And drama is created by excess thinking and storytelling. In the end, you just don't feel good and relaxed, which is what you're aiming for.

In dramatic and unhealthy relationships, this happens again and again. You are creating the drama by what you deem acceptable or unacceptable in a relationship or friendship. To attract less drama, it's important to be aware of this dynamic and then move away from it and toward peace. It's also important not to try to fix it, because dramatic people often can't be *fixed* until they decide to on their own.

How Drama Creates Trauma

I define being traumatized as the occurrence of a single event or repetition of events that alters your way of thinking about yourself and the world. Dramatic relationships and their endings become deeply embedded in our psyche and affect how we interact with others in the future.

For example, imagine you're a woman dating a man who is a football fanatic. On Sunday afternoon, your partner gets into a fight with his friends over a football game. You don't particularly care about football, but he comes home in a huff. Being a compassionate person, you try to console him. You say, "It's only a game— don't get so upset about it." But then he gets mad at you. He says, "Why do you always cut me down for liking football? Lots of people like football!" Now it's an argument about how you belittle his interests. Then he calls you stupid.

This has nothing to do with you. It has to do with him, his friends, and his issues. But you get pulled into his drama vortex. And then you feel bad and punish yourself by canceling a Sunday dinner with your girl-friends.

And then the pattern continues. You start walking on eggshells more. You start acting differently around him. Perhaps you start saying less and remaining quiet when the two of you argue. Then you start blaming yourself more for the problems in the relationship. You start thinking you need to be more sensitive to his needs. But this is all bullshit. What you are really saying is, "If I am more sensitive, he will get angry less." And now you're in an abusive relationship. This happens all the time, by the way, to varying degrees.

And why did all this happen? Because you cared for him and wanted him to feel better after a football game.

Remember, you were just being kind because you wanted him to feel better. But you got pulled into his drama, mostly due to lack of awareness.

Seek Out Meaningful Experiences

I call drama the fast food of relationships. It's tasty and quick, and it tricks your mind into thinking you have just experienced something substantial.

Dramatic relationships are *not* meaningful, but the mind mistakes them for meaningful because they are emotionally intense. You need to be aware of this.

A meaningful event is when your grandmother whom you deeply care for dies and you attend her funeral, or one of your best friends whom you haven't seen in a year returns to town, and the two of you discuss life over coffee all Saturday afternoon. These are the powerful events that shape your life.

Conversely, a dramatic event is when you lend your partner your car and he or she totals it. Now you have no way to get to work. It's emotionally intense but not because it's meaningful but rather because it's dramatic and messes up your life.

You can differentiate between meaningful and dramatic by asking this simple question when an event happens: "Do I want to be here or not?" At your grandmother's funeral, the answer would be yes. At the po-

lice station bailing out your soon-to-be "ex," the answer
would be no.

Move toward events in your life that are meaningful
and away from the dramatic ones, and your life will go
much more smoothly.

How to Move Forward in a Relationship

The final reason to avoid drama in a relationship is
that it prevents forward movement in your life. If you
are always in conflict with your partner around money,
your relationship, or how to raise your kids, it's hard to
get anything done. Constant drama only results in a side-
to-side relationship motion. The boat is rocking back
and forth, but you aren't going anywhere. Your relationship is stuck, with little hope of advancing to a deeper,
more intimate level because you can't move forward to
get there.

So if you avoid all drama, does that mean a relationship will no longer be exciting?

There is always going to be some drama in a relationship. But when you minimize the theatrics, you stop the
white noise that prevents you from having a real con-
nection with your partner. There is a natural way of relating and connecting with a person that emerges when
drama is reduced. You begin to authentically relate to
each other, not through your mental stories but rather

from a place of love and peace. You find new, more exciting ways to support each other. And you laugh together more as new experiences become possible.

Drama is not healthy. It is intense and interesting but doesn't truly give you what you deeply seek. Instead, you get pulled into other people's stories and never get to experience a truly loving, supportive relationship. Try to avoid drama. Instead, seek a caring, loving individual who likes being with you for who you are, and skip all the explosions and gunpowder.

CHAPTER 2

Take the Tinfoil Off Your Head

Strategy #2
Don't Project Your Beliefs onto Others

The mind does an interesting thing when you walk into a coffee shop full of people. It projects all your beliefs and assumptions onto everyone else in the room, even if you have never met them before. You are not aware you are doing this, but you are.

What Eastern philosophy and Buddhism call illusion is really what you do when you walk into any coffee shop. You load up a reality in your head of how you think people should behave and also how you should behave.

Most likely you expect customers to wait in line and not cut in front of you. You expect the staff to be pleasant, not rude, when taking your order. And you expect them to actually make a coffee for you, not throw a dishrag in your face and tell you to do the dishes in the back.

All this helps reduce stress by making the world around you seem predictable.

Everything works smoothly as long as no one breaks the rules.

For example, I'm a friendly person, so I expect others to be friendly as well. When I order coffee at Starbucks, I expect the staff to be pleasant and engaging when taking my order. If my server is instead dismissive and rude, I'll walk away from the experience upset. I might even think about talking to the manager and complaining about the poor customer service I received.

Because I'm friendly, I expect (and have a strong belief) that others should be the same. And when they do not share my belief, it challenges my belief system.

Still Remembering the Jerk from the Party

I shared an example in the last chapter of being at a party where someone insults you. You remember the person because he or she created an unpleasant emotional experience for you.

But the other reason is that the individual has a different belief system from you. Your belief system states that at a party, everyone will attempt to be pleasant and friendly. You expect everyone else to have secretly agreed to this belief. But someone else could hold a very different belief. He or she could come to the party thinking, "I'm going to insult as many people as possible at this party." When the two of you collide, sparks fly.

Projecting Your Beliefs onto Your Partner Leads to Disaster

Nowhere is projecting our beliefs on others more of a problem than in dating and relationships. When we first meet someone we like, whether in person or online, our mind automatically begins to try to get them to fit into our worldview.

If your mind uses this process when you run out to grab a cup of coffee, can you imagine how much more it does it when you are assessing a potential mate? We will unconsciously project many of our beliefs and expectations on them. As you can imagine, making the mistake of assuming that you and your partner share the same belief system can lead to a variety of problems, especially after you have put your heart into the relationship. To avoid this, have frank conversations at the beginning of a relationship about important issues in order to avoid being blindsided by something that goes against your values and beliefs in the end.

Three Exercises

Write down as many answers to these questions as possible. Ignore the usual politically correct responses and focus on your deepest desires and needs. It is not uncommon for me to work with strong, independent women who would like a partner who will also take care of them so they can relax. If you need to go against a perceived feminine or masculine code, do so. Reflect deeply on what you truly want, whatever that is. If you want a loving provider, ask for that. If you want a mate who will share everything with you equally (e.g., chores, money), ask for that.

Ask for what you want without guilt. In this way, you are clear, direct, and honest with yourself, and you communicate more clearly with any future mates. Life is easier that way.

Question #1

In a relationship with me, my partner has to be:

Skip the ideas of attractive, intelligent, sporty, funny, etc., which are obvious when you first meet someone. List relationship qualities that you cannot necessarily see when you walk into the coffee shop on that first date.

Examples include: loving, caring, truthful, emotionally supportive, kind, generous, values saving money, independent, responsible, a good communicator, family oriented, sensual, passionate, excited about being in a relationship.

Question #2

What is <u>so obvious</u> to me that I require from a partner that I wouldn't even think to ask?

These are the deeper qualities you have that you *assume* the person has just because you have them yourself. You need to ask (or discover through the dating process) whether a person does indeed have these other qualities *before* getting seriously involved with him or her. It'll be much more painful to find out later that he or she doesn't.

Examples include: Doesn't cheat on me. Makes me the number one priority in his life. Wants to have children. Wants to have fun. Wants to have a short-term relationship only. Wants to get married eventually. Is financially pragmatic.

You may have to think about this question for a little while because I'm asking you to see your blind spots. Your blind spots are the aspects of your personality that you don't see that cause you to attract a specific type of person repeatedly.

Also, think back to your childhood and reflect on it. We get our first model of how we should be in relationship from our parents, whether we like it or not. Don't judge it as good or bad—just observe any tendencies or unconscious assumptions you might be carrying based on your upbringing.

For example, if you had a really safe and supportive childhood, you might automatically assume that all relationships will be safe and loving. If you had an abusive childhood, you might assume that all relationships will be abusive, no matter who you date.

Many of my clients are one of two types. Those who didn't have a great upbringing and who survived some sort of abuse. They tend to repeat that pattern with the people they date.

Others had healthy upbringings but end up dating jerks anyway. These people are what I call my "They never saw that person coming" group. They really didn't. If your upbringing was loving and supportive, you would not expect a person to lie and manipulate you in a relationship. It's just not your reality. Only later, once you're deep in the relationship, do you discover that you're dating a monster. Then it's a hard road back.

A final key point: some questions you can't just ask because everyone will say no. Avoid asking questions like "Are you going to cheat on me?" or "Are you going to take all my money and buy a new pickup truck with it?" (True story.) People are not going to answer yes to those questions. They might not even know that they will do those things. As far as questions go, get a history of their past relationships over time. Just don't interrogate them! And remember, people can change if they put in the work and can become more aware of themselves.

Question #3

What is it I've never had in a partner before?
Or feel embarrassed or guilty to ask for?

Make a list:

This is a great question to help you become more aware of what you are having trouble receiving in a relationship so you can ask for it in the future. To receive these new qualities in a partner, you have to realize you are worthy of receiving them. You don't have to be any better than you are right now to get them—not more attractive, more intelligent, or more successful.

The reason we often do not attract exactly what we want in a mate is simply because we don't think we deserve it, we feel guilty for asking, or we think we have to become better first. We don't. Nothing need be fixed before happiness can occur.

I want you to be blown away by the kind of mate you can attract. Let go of your self-limiting beliefs and go for gold.

So dig deep and ask for what you really desire. Seek your happiest relationship and that's what you'll get. You can have whatever you want.

Visit www.TheRelationshipCode.com to access all your bonus material, including your *free* online course.

Chapter 3

Blind Trust, or Relationships for Lazy People

In dating, trust is very important. You want to be able to relax and trust someone with your heart.

But sometimes we trust someone and end up getting hurt. We then question why we trusted them in the first place.

But the real question is: was that person you trusted always going to hurt you?

The answer is yes.

The reason is that the expectations you had of that person were not based on who they *really* were, but rather on who you *hoped* they were. When push came to shove, the person you hoped they were underneath was not there. Disappointment and pain usually follow this realization. It can be heartbreaking.

People are creatures of habit, and our past often dictates our future. However, this truth is often ignored when dating someone.

Instead, we turn a blind eye to some of their personality traits, their childhood history, and their relationship history, thinking we won't be affected by them. We will.

This is what I call blind trust—trusting someone more than you should based on how they present themselves. In fact, everyone is showing you exactly how they will be in a relationship the moment you meet them. Are they on time or late? Are they talkative or a person of few words? Do they check their phone constantly? Do they avoid confrontation or lean into it? Are they sensitive or dismissive of your emotions?

Unfortunately, we ignore most of it because we don't want our ideal vision of this person disrupted.

Call it being idealistic or lazy, but either way, you are not observing and questioning a potential mate to see if that person is truly a good fit for you. You are just hoping that when the time comes, he or she will do the right thing (the thing you want to happen) rather than the one that has a 99 percent chance of happening.

For example, you date a guy who was an alcoholic or someone who has cheated on mates in the past. He says he has learned his lesson and that it will not be a problem with you. Be aware: it most likely will be a problem with you.

Maybe you think everyone can change. It's okay to have that attitude, but just don't get disappointed when people don't.

Human behavior is mostly predictable. A person's past tends to repeat itself, creating the same future. The problem is that we believe a person's words above everything else and get disappointed when their words don't match their behavior. How many times have you made a New Year's resolution to go to the gym and lose weight? Did you go?

By observing someone's personality and behavior, it's not really that hard to guess how they will be with you.

You might be better off dating someone who says, "I drink a lot and that's probably not going to change, and I'll probably sleep with someone else." That seems like a surprisingly more relaxed relationship, and at least you'll go into it with your eyes open.

At some level, we are all optimistic. We want to give people a chance, but we have to give the right people a chance. As previously mentioned, people are creatures of habit. And what they have done in the past endlessly repeats until they break the cycle on their own through acceptance, insight, positive choice, and sustainable action.

I have tried the blind trust approach many times, and

it has never worked out.

I would argue that most of the suffering that occurs in relationships is not because of the way a person is but rather because of the way we are hoping they will be—but never are.

This doesn't mean that you become super-critical of everyone; what it does mean is that you truly accept the person as he or she is when you first meet him or her and see where it goes from there. You avoid looking at only the good points and tuning out all the bad ones, thinking they won't be a big deal. At some point, they will be.

Four Tips to Minimize Blind Trust

1) Discover the way the person was before you started dating him or her.

This most likely is how he or she will be in a relationship with you. Assume this first and work backward. Better to be pleasantly surprised that the person changed than devastated that he or she didn't.

What is this person's relationship like with family and friends? How did things end with ex-partners? You can learn a lot about a person by learning about his or her relationships with friends, family, and past partners.

How is this person with money? If this person is bad with money, is he or she working on it? How is this person with cleaning up his or her place?

Accept as much as you can and decide if, given what you see, you can move forward. This is just a light starting point, not the Spanish Inquisition, but having a sense of the person's tendencies right away will limit surprises when dating.

2) Take note of how the person is treating you right now.

Let this be your baseline. If the person is treating you well, expect (and, in fact, demand) that you always be treated this way, regardless of the length of the relationship. I don't believe in a honeymoon period. It always has to be good. You also have to be able to recognize being treated well by someone who is just trying to make a good impression but isn't really that way underneath. Follow your intuition.

Also, look for multiple positive qualities, not just a single big one. For example, you start dating someone who likes to take the lead in a relationship. Maybe your last partner was a bit of a pushover. That's great, but don't assume that someone who takes the lead is also someone who will treat you well long-term. These are two different qualities in a partner. Look for each one separately.

An example of "ignoring the obvious" that I often hear from my clients is dating someone who is always too busy at work and is never really available. This person keeps saying that once things settle down, he or she will have more time for the relationship. Oftentimes this pattern never changes, and the person will always be too busy, so if you are not okay with that, let it go.

Always ensure that you are getting your needs met now, not in some fictional future. Your happiness and fulfillment in the present moment are the greatest indicators of your future happiness in this relationship. As I often tell my clients, "If you're happy with the way the person is treating you now and that continues, why would that relationship end?"

3) *Observe how the person treats people he or she sees as having little perceived value.*

Whenever I take a woman out on a date, I observe how she treats panhandlers on the street and the serving staff at the restaurant where we are dining. Is she kind to these people as well?

If your date treats people well who are seen as being of low value in society, you know you are dating someone good.

The underlying reasoning for this is that your partner is going to try to impress you on a date because he or she is interested in you. But how does this person treat the people he or she doesn't care about impressing?

How your date treats those people will be how *you* will be treated when he or she is really angry at you or doesn't care about your opinion anymore.

Don't expect that you are always going to be on the good side of the tracks with this person. This is also why I like to know if a woman ended her last relationship in a mature way. Was she still civil when she realized the relationship was over? This is a measure of true character.

I always find it worrisome when someone tells me, "I heard he can be very disrespectful, but he treats me very well, so I'm not worried about it." You're on borrowed time with that relationship because eventually you will be on the other side of the tracks.

I've heard of the opposite situation, where a person treats everyone else but his or her partner well, so you want to avoid that situation as well.

Not everyone is going to be perfect, and I'm not asking you to look for a combination of Gandhi, King Arthur, and Brad Pitt or Audrey Hepburn, but use these tips as a starting point to ferret out some of the problematic people on the front end in order to make your life easier on the back end.

4) Find out for yourself.

Sometime friends and family will recommend someone and say that person is a great catch. They want you to be married and settle down. It's important to discover for yourself if someone is worth your time, regardless of what everyone else thinks. You have to discover the truth for yourself. It is your life and your happiness that are at stake.

Real Trust: Trust That Has Been Gained Over Time Through Experiences

So if we no longer rely on blind trust, what do we do? We learn how to trust a person based on our experiences with him or her. This is what I call real trust.

Real trust is based on the way a person is and how he or she behaves with you over time. This knowledge and awareness allow you to safely trust a person at a deeper level and experience fewer surprises.

You also need to trust your intuition. Can you feel that this person is trustworthy in your heart and are not simply being hopeful in your mind?

I'm not saying everyone needs to be perfect, as we are always working on ourselves, but over time you should be getting a deeper sense of whether or not you can really rely on someone.

For example, if you are dating someone who is very

open and honest with his or her feelings, you have a solid indicator of how the relationship will be in the future. With real trust, you are seeing the real personality of someone and are speculating less, which leads to less heartbreak.

I often tell my clients, "If they wouldn't do it in Cirque de Soleil, don't do it when dating."

At Cirque, skilled acrobats are trained to catch each other 50 feet in the air. When an acrobat is flying through the air with no net, he or she is not thinking, "Gee, I hope this person catches me."

That would be blind trust.

Visit www.TheRelationshipCode.com to access all your bonus material, including your *free* online course.

CHAPTER 4

Let's Open Up
This Can of Worms

Strategy #4
Be Open and Authentic
When Meeting Someone

Being open and authentic is a key aspect of finding happiness in a relationship and in life. When you are real, not only is it easier, but you will also attract the same caliber of people and be able to recognize the fakes who are just giving you a line.

Being as authentic and genuine as possible when you first meet someone allows you to not only have a better time when you first get together but also discern how authentic the other person really is.

Working with a client, I was told how he and his wife were on their best behavior for the first six months of dating. His belief was that you can't be yourself when you begin dating because you would never stay together.

So you trick yourself and the other person into thinking the relationship is better than it actually is, only to find out later that neither of you is really satisfied. The goal is not to get into *any* relationship—it is to get into the *right* one.

Be as clear as you can from the start. This is possible by being relaxed and at ease with who you are and with what has happened in your life previously. The value of this approach is that open, authentic people recognize each other because they interact in the same way.

Often when we meet someone, especially on the first couple of dates, we pretend to be more interesting than we actually are. Never do this. *Be real, be broken, be happy, be normal.*

It's common at the beginning of a relationship to not feel that being yourself is enough. In fact, you're more than enough.

If a date goes sour, most likely it was because you did not allow enough of your personality out to create a noticeable difference and to wake the other person up to the real and amazing you (or they were just looking for someone to complete their story).

In general, most of us wear some type of mask when we begin seeing someone, especially if it's someone we immediately like. We try to be overly polite and perhaps overly nice when in fact we need to create a little bit of conscious trouble.

The heart needs to beat a little faster to see if something is possible. There has to be a waking up out of the doldrums of life. Being bold and authentic can do this with surprising results for you and your date. Be bold. Be loving. Be fully you.

However, being bold does not mean you need to be super extroverted and outspoken. If that is not you, don't do it. Bold means being bold for who you are. Maybe you are more of the quiet type and like to listen to others. In that case, being bolder at a party would mean not judging yourself but instead really enjoying listening and smiling at people in response to the stories they tell you.

Perhaps you are an artist, write poetry, or love to cook, exercise, or read. Share that part of you more. Be unconventional and surprises await. Most of us have a narrow vision of what is supposed to work in a relationship and what doesn't. Many of our ideas come from what we see on TV and what is popular and trending in mainstream media. Big gestures, steamy sex, big breasts, and fancy lingerie. Overt and explicit, these pictures and sounds have no subtlety and very little to do with real life.

How do you capture the quietest whisper between two lovers, the moving of a glass that your partner almost knocks off the table, or laughing hysterically with each other when something goes terribly wrong?

If we only did what we see on TV or read in magazines, no one would ever whisper, sex would always be on the first date, the guy would have ripped abs, and the girl would be perfect. Nobody would ever have bad breath, pass gas, or feel insecure about anything. People would be confident, loud, and outspoken. And everyone would have a perfect job. This is not only an illusion but also rather boring.

Give me that for a day or two, and then it's time to leave Rodeo Drive and surrender to the beauty of being real and sharing the imperfectness of two people (or however many people you want to date).

There are many powerful gestures we can share, but we have to be our authentic self to do so. If we limit ourself based on what we think we should be doing or sharing, we have already lost. It's about sharing honestly and not judging ourself too harshly or worrying about how our actions might be perceived. We don't really know until we try.

I once dated a girl who was an artist and made me a handmade birthday card with a sweet saying on the back. I loved that gift, framed it, and kept it for years. I told her that one day, and she was so surprised. Although it was a small gesture to her, it was very special to me because no one had ever made me anything like that before.

I remember being touched by a woman I was in a relationship with who made me bag lunches before going to work. This may seem small, but for someone who has been on his own awhile, having a homemade lunch made by someone else can be quite a nice addition to your day. The point is that you don't know the impact you can have on others just by being you. If you filter that out because you "think" it's not how you are supposed to be, you might miss out on affecting someone in a way you could never have imagined. So be yourself.

We can also get caught up in feeling obliged to follow "dating rules." What should we talk about, how many dates should we have before we kiss or sleep together. Now, while I don't want you throwing out all the rules of civil engagement, like showing up unshowered and in your housecoat on your first date, dating rules should be held lightly. My own experiences and those of some of my clients who have made good relationship connections are similar. The rules of engagement went out the window. See each other for the next three days in a row. Bring the person home and cook him or her dinner, and then have fun. Get away for the weekend. Do what you want—not what you think you "should" be doing. When both people are happy and into it, don't let some canned rules prevent you from living life to the fullest. That's what dating and relationships are for. Embrace the opportunities and don't be too squeamish.

Now, let me clarify a few points about being authentic. Most people think they are being authentic when in fact they are just rambling on. Authenticity is truly you just being you and fully expressing yourself in the present moment. It is not reactive, and it is not numbed out. Authenticity has a natural openness to it. There's a softness and powerfulness to it at the same time. When you are authentic, you sometimes startle yourself because you didn't even know what you were going to say next.

There will be a spontaneity to your words and actions, and in that unplanned moment something new and exciting emerges if you let it.

Some people are pretty boring to talk with. Just have a conversation for an hour with someone on an airplane and you'll find a lot of tedious and repetitious talk. When someone is authentic and open to new things, they have a lot of energy and seem excited about things. They listen to new ideas and are enthusiastic about your passions.

One of my dearest relationships was with a woman with whom this happened all the time. We would have conversations and adjust our positions based on what the other person was saying. It wasn't only about defending a position—it was about listening and being open to changing our opinions based on what was happening in the moment. Interestingly, our intimacy deepened each time we had one of these conversations because we connected more deeply through the learning experience.

This was much different from the conversations I had with the yoga instructor I referred to in the introduction. We had many arguments and discussions, and she would never adjust her position. She was always looking to confirm what she already believed—that I was a liar and was untrustworthy (she had experienced this type of person in her past) even though I constantly tried to tell her I was not.

Sometimes people believe they are being genuine when, in fact, they are being a bit lazy in a relationship. Being real does not mean, "I don't care how I look or what I say, so take it or leave it." You always need to put positive intention into something to get good rewards. As well, brutal honesty has nothing to do with authenticity. Telling people off, unloading on them, or saying everything that comes to mind when angry only reveals a person who is too immature to deal with his or her personal issues.

And finally, some people will use the approach of being tough or not caring as a technique to draw in a partner—the "playing hard to get" strategy. Don't do this. This approach does not use natural attraction principles such as authenticity, openness, and compatibility. It is about mind games and playing with human physiology to manufacture a desire to be closer with someone through push-and-pull dynamics. It holds little water when determining the true nature of a partner. (It is best used for fun when you are looking for some quick sex or just flirting at the bar.)

Notice how a person responds to you. It is not only being your true self that can establish a good relationship but also how your date behaves. Does he or she shut you down by being closed and rigid? Does your date say things that are boring or that give the impression that he or she is playing a role or reciting a formula from past dates? Does he or she say everything you want to hear but comes across as a little too smooth? If so, you may want to pass on that person, even if there is an initial attraction.

Ultimately, if you or your partner cannot be truly authentic and genuine and are not willing to work on the relationship, perhaps now is not the time to commit. The relationship code is about having integrity and being true to who you are and to that special someone you wish to be with. (And please note, integrity does not mean you don't have any fun.)

Attracting a powerful and amazing relationship is also about moving through your own stuff so you can be open to receiving someone better than you have been with in the past. Be happy, be yourself, accept who you are, share your unique self, and see what happens.

Visit www.TheRelationshipCode.com to access all your bonus material, including your *free* online course.

CHAPTER 5

Why You Date Someone You Fit With, Not Someone You Like

Have you ever been at a party or some other event and seen a couple who look totally wrong for each other?

Perhaps one is loud and boorish, and the other is quiet and worrying. Perhaps one is watching what he or she eats and is health conscious, and the other is eating and drinking everything in sight. And you think, "Why are they together?"

And then in your mind, do you construct a reason? "He probably has lots of money." "She sleeps around." "He has low self-esteem."

The reason is not any of those things. We are drawn to our opposite in order to feel complete within ourselves. Nature abhors a vacuum, so we are always looking to create a sense of wholeness in how we experience the world. This is nowhere more apparent than in relationships.

If one person is quicker to anger, you'll often find the other one is quieter and more understanding. If someone has a dramatic life, the other one will have a calmer, more orderly life.

Often when we are attracted to someone, it is because he or she has an opposite energy (or personality). Opposing energies create good chemistry.

If you mix water and water together, you simply get more water. This is great for love and compatibility, but it doesn't always create the "pop"' of drama we like to feel in the moment when dating someone new.

The "pop" that occurs with our opposite makes us feel alive and excited. You will unconsciously rule out potential mates if they do not cause you to "pop" in some way.

Here is an exercise to see how this works in your own life.

For a week, become mindful of how you interact with someone at home (or at work or in a coffee shop) and notice how you strive to keep things balanced with that person. Perhaps he or she dominates conversations, so you fill in the space as the listener, trying to find a balance with that person to keep the conversation going. Or if you don't care about balance, notice how the other person strives to maintain balance with you. Typically, there will be a more static individual and a more dynamic individual in all conversations. Which one are you?

That's how physical chemistry binds us to another on an unconscious level. However, just because you feel an attraction doesn't mean this person is necessarily good for you.

And the more opposite you are to your partner (opposites attract, as you know), the greater the chemistry you will have with the person and the more addictive the relationship will become. An example is the classic nice girl/bad boy scenario.

Unfortunately, while a short-term relationship like this can be super sexy, long-term it will fall flat. For a long-term relationship to be successful, you need to be more similar to your partner than you are different.

People who have mutual goals, beliefs, and dreams are able to create a relationship reality that works well for both of them. They are moving in the same direction throughout their time together. In the end, this means you both have to be more like water to combine, flow, and grow together in the relationship.

Why Relationships End

Almost all relationships we are in, at least when we are younger, are based on this chemistry we have with the person we are dating. We think we are making a choice to be with someone, but we are not—we're glued to the other person because of the "opposites attract energy," being pulled along and simply enjoying the feeling.

A relationship ends when the chemistry between the two of you (the "opposites attract energy") no longer works with the type of relationship you want to be in. A classic example is when you meet someone and are dating casually. You socialize a lot together, sleep together, and really enjoy each other's company. At some point, one of you wants to get serious. If the other person doesn't, the relationship is on borrowed time.

Think of it like a guitar string, and you and your partner are the two points of attachment. When a guitar string is attached on both ends, you get a note. If both of you find that note pleasant, you start dating.

When you adjust the tension you are putting on the string, either by pulling it harder, giving it slack, or moving your end of the string across the fretboard, the note changes. Ultimately, the other person also has to adjust his or her position to stay tuned with you (in other words, he or she must also want to change the type of relationship the two of you are in).

But the other person may not be interested in this adjustment or might not have the ability to change.

If one or both people aren't conscious enough to adjust to this new relationship, or if one of them just doesn't want to, the relationship will end. In that case, there is nothing you can do to salvage it unless you change your insertion point.

We often look at how the guitar string is being played, such as the movement of the hand across the string, to judge the quality of a relationship. But we seldom consider the attachment points as being key to the sound that is created.

A lot of heartbreak occurs because we simply do not see and accept this principle.

Think back to a hurtful breakup, and you will see that something happened, the situation changed, you changed or he or she changed, and then the dynamic shifted and the relationship died. The note could no longer be played, or you wanted to play a new note that your partner couldn't (or didn't want to).

It happens. You grasped onto something you didn't understand like two kids hanging on and spinning on a merry-go-round. It's fun, but then someone lets go or falls off. There's no one to blame.

Simply accept this. It was always going to end this way, whether you liked it or not.

I often see this in couples counseling where, after several years in the marriage, one partner wants the other to communicate better or be more involved in the relationship. While it might seem like a reasonable request, the person he or she married was often not a good communicator in the first place. I then teach the couple to: a) accept the person they married, b) determine if they want to stay together, and c) discover how to do that in a new way that is both conscious and loving.

How to Date Someone You Truly Like

The title of this chapter is *Why You Date Someone You Fit With, Not Someone You Like*. When you date someone who is your opposite, you do not actually like that person on his or her own; you like the person because he or she is different from you.

A loud, bold person might like a quiet, sensitive person. This is attraction through contrast. I myself have had the experience of really liking someone and then breaking up and thinking, "What did I ever see in that person? She wasn't very nice."

(This is, of course, when your friends say, "We told you that! But you wouldn't listen.")

When you were with the person, you complemented each other due to your differences. And when you were two parts of a whole person in the relationship, you couldn't see it because you were too heavily addicted to the chemistry, drama, and great sex.

These qualities aren't indicators of a truly compatible person. You need both chemistry and compatibility for a relationship to be sustainable. Typically, I look for 20 percent chemistry and 80 percent compatibility for long-term relationship potential (though you can play with the numbers, depending on your goals). A compatible person is someone who is more similar to you than different. You have similar views and beliefs about the world and similar interests. You like the person *not* because he or she is different from you but because he or she is similar to you. And should the relationship end, you still like the person afterward.

So why is it easier to find someone you are opposite to instead of someone who you are similar to? The reason is that you must love the qualities you have within yourself before you can love them in another.

Only when you fully embrace and accept the wonderful qualities in yourself will you be able to find them in another. We live in a world where we tend to reject (or undervalue) who we are and overvalue who we are not. If you think, for example, that being introverted is a poor trait instead of something beautiful, you will be more impressed when you see someone at a party who is very outspoken. You'll think, "I want to be more like him." In truth, if you ignored the extrovert, you might actually see the love of your life listening quietly beside you.

Self-esteem is accepting and valuing who you are without judgment and seeking out other similar people. Birds of a feather flock together. And they have a lot of fun laying eggs.

Of course, that's not the end of it. You also have a duty to complete yourself as a human being—to make yourself into a whole person who is not limited by his or her old beliefs or past conditioning. You can be an introvert and still enjoy going out and talking to new people. The reason that we are only half of ourselves in the first place and attract our opposite is because we have a self-limiting belief that we cannot embody opposite qualities within ourselves at the same time. The tough guy doesn't think he can show vulnerability, and the nice girl doesn't feel she can say in mixed company that she really enjoys sex.

If the tough guy could also show his vulnerability and the nice girl could embrace her sexuality without feeling guilty, those two people would no longer attract the opposite energy and would no longer have to live vicariously through another person. They would attract someone more similar to them and enjoy a much more compatible relationship.

So complete yourself. Make the parts of you that you are consciously or unconsciously rejecting more welcome and integrated parts of you.

In the end, it all works out if you keep working to become more self-aware: you date opposites, date people who are compatible, and eventually find someone who fits perfectly in the middle.

Visit www.TheRelationshipCode.com to access all your bonus material, including your *free* online course.

CHAPTER 6

Wishful Thinking, or Why You Should Buy the Convertible Instead

Strategy #6
Don't Assume Your Relationship Will Magically Improve

Nowhere in my counseling practice do I see less fruitful behavior than hanging on to poor relationships because you just hope things will get better.

Wishful thinking is hoping the person you are with right now will become a better partner (or that the relationship will magically improve) if you do nothing about it and just wait.

Wishful thinking is hoping that the two of you not having sex or constantly arguing over finances will not affect the long-term success of your relationship. Wishful thinking causes you to not act when you need to act.

In a sense, wishful thinking is not being in a relationship with the person who is right in front of you but instead dating the person you hope the other person will be.

A classic example (and sad situation) I see in my practice is a woman who is having an affair with a married man. The man keeps promising that he will eventually leave his wife, but he never does. The woman is using wishful thinking to keep the relationship going. In her mind, she sees them blissfully happy together in the not-too-distant future. She stays in the relationship not because she likes the current situation but because she envisions a better one. She is seeing no evidence of this, however. The husband is not initiating divorce proceedings with his wife, even though he has been unhappy for the last ten years.

Another situation is someone who is dating a workaholic. The person keeps promising that he or she will spend more time together once things slow down at work. But months go by, even years, and the situation stays the same. The partner puts up with not being in a satisfying relationship because of the magical future when the two people have lots of free time to spend together, but it never arrives.

There is a reason this happens so frequently. People are creatures of habit, and it requires far fewer mental and emotional resources to stay the same than it does to change. Even if a person is very unhappy at work or in a relationship, it is still easier to stay the course. It's easier to live a life of quiet desperation than to choose happiness.

Happiness is not for the faint of heart.

Whenever you start any relationship, you must always take it at face value. You must accept it "as it is" right now. If it is a short-term fling, accept it as such. If it is only a friendship, become friends. If you are having an affair, accept it for what it is and don't think you are going to run away together. If both people are open and fully available for a relationship, go for it.

Wishful thinking can take several forms:

1) Hoping the person you are dating right now will change

2) Hoping that the relationship situation you are in will change (for example, one person wants no commitment and the other wants marriage; one wants to start a family and the other doesn't want children)

3) Hoping you don't have to change yourself to get a better result in a relationship (for example, you avoid working on your self-confidence or jealously issues)

4) Hoping that if you just ignore the issue, it will not become a bigger problem in the future. I see this especially with couples who have decided to stay in the

marriage for the children's sake and are now living as roommates (no sex). Eventually one of them comes across someone in the outside world who makes them feel like an attractive human being again, and an affair happens. It was always going to happen—it was just a matter of time.

Let me give you an example from my own life. I began a relationship with someone, and we started talking about our compatibility. She told me straight out, "I have difficulties trusting men."

Now, when someone says something like that or something like "People always betray me," you should run away as quickly as possible because right up front that person is telling you exactly what your relationship is going to be like.

Unfortunately, most of us are too egotistical (or blindly optimistic) to receive this valuable information and end it there. Instead, we think to ourselves, "I am different" or "I'll show you what it's like to be with someone who treats you well and will change your mind." This will not happen because *it has nothing to do with you.*

You are not so special that you can change this person, nor should you. Why? Because, as I mentioned before, people don't want to change. They prefer to stay the same and continue to confirm what they have already experienced in their past.

As I often tell my clients, you can affect people, but the change is up to them.

So what was my response to this lady when she told me she didn't trust men? "Don't worry—we can work on that!"

And that was the reason we broke up—because no matter what I did, she never trusted me.

Now, I'm not trying to be pessimistic about relationships, but what I want you to do is to date and clearly see who is right in front of you—both the amazing aspects and the flawed ones. I don't want you to date or be in a relationship with a person based on who you would like him or her to be but is not. You will have fewer surprises and be able to take that relationship exactly where you know it can go, not somewhere it won't.

People can change, and relationships can shift, but it can be difficult if the two of you are too different and don't share the same long-term vision.

Sometimes we buy a car and later wish we had bought the convertible instead or got a different color. Relationships are like that, too. We get into a relationship but then wish it were different. But most cars can't be upgraded after you buy them. You have what you have. Just enjoy it and skip the buyer's remorse. That's not to say you shouldn't want to be in an upgraded relationship, but sometimes it can't happen with the person you're with.

The final topic I want to talk about in this chapter is accepting personal responsibility for your part in any relationship you are in. A friend of mine who is a spiritual coach and relationship adviser always says that no matter what the issue, it's 50 percent one person's fault and 50 percent the other's. I was resistant to this concept initially (especially in abusive situations) but now I know it to be true.

It is important to understand that whenever we are dating or in a serious relationship, it is the dynamic that occurs between the two individuals that creates the problem. It is never just one person's fault.

When you are in a relationship, you are always 50 percent responsible for what is happening in it. You are always making choices about what you are going to put up with or not put up with. You are choosing to cause or not cause trouble, to be kind or unkind, to be open to receiving love or rejecting it. You are 50 percent of the dynamic.

Two people are needed to create a dynamic. This is a very powerful realization, not a depressing one, because by changing you, you can change the dynamic of any relationship. I have seen astounding results from couples I've worked with where one person changed the way he or she was interacting with a partner, and the relationship went from stalled to totally amazing! They both finally had the dynamic they always wanted with their partner.

People want to be happy—we just don't know what we are doing sometimes. Within this book, I'm giving you the tools to create a great relationship for yourself.

Final Thoughts on Wishful Thinking

We are all in the process of learning and becoming more conscious. We all have different conditions that originate from our childhood, our personality style, and things we have picked up along the way. You bring all of that to any relationship you are in. But you must accept the power you have to change things—to make yourself a better person and allow any relationship to prosper.

Just remember that hoping for happiness does not just lead to happiness. You have to address things along the way.

Visit www.TheRelationshipCode.com to access all your bonus material, including your *free* online course.

CHAPTER 7

Ask and You May Receive

> *Strategy #7*
> Ask for What You Want
> in a Relationship

One of the key aspects of being happy in a relation-ship is being able to ask for what you want. Un-fortunately, most of us have a tendency to feel guilty for asking or expect the other person to say no.

But asking for what you want and being able to re-ceive it are key aspects of finding happiness in any re-lationship.

Here are six ways to get more of what you want:

1. Appreciate what you have

Any relationship you are in has a level of abundance to it. There are good things, and there are bad things. Focus on the good things. When you focus on the prob-lems, you get out of your heart and can't really see what the other person is trying to offer you right now.

Instead of criticizing your partner, try this: slow down your breathing and focus on your heart. This will take you out of your head and bring you more into your body and the present moment once again. When this happens, you will be able to much more easily sense the person and be able to appreciate him or her just for being there.

Not only will this allow you to connect more deeply with your partner, but you will also be able to appreciate the person for just being him- or herself. Every person is so unique!

You'll soon discover that there is a lot more being offered by this person than you had previously thought, even though it doesn't necessarily fit the mold of what you thought this person was going to give you.

2. Ask for what you want and expect a "yes" in return

We often have a fear of asking for what we want. We think we are being a bother or don't want to expose ourselves by risking a request. Also, we can have expectations without being considered a controlling person.

If you never ask for what you want, how can you get it?

Moreover, when you hold back from asking, you never actually find out what your partner is truly capable of giving you. Instead, you live up in your head, saying to yourself, "Oh, he or she probably wouldn't do that anyway." But you don't know because you never asked.

Also if you don't ask, resentment can build up, especially if it is something you truly desire in a relationship.

I often find in my private practice that people want to connect more deeply and give much more to their partner but just don't know how. Asking for what you want helps with this process.

This approach can be especially difficult if you were brought up in an abusive environment or were taught to always put someone else's needs before your own. If you were in a previous relationship in which your partner made you feel ashamed about your needs, it can be difficult to ask your next partner for the same thing. But you must be bold and ask anyway, and challenge your learned response. You have to ask and see what is available. Just expect a positive response.

Don't, however, ask in an overly demanding way. Instead, come from a place of openness and vulnerability. This is the best approach. You will often be surprised at how many people want to please you when you ask from your heart.

3. Be clear to your partner about the consequences of not getting your needs met

There will be times in a relationship when you are not getting what you want. Even though I talk about only being with people who are genuine, that does not mean the person you are with doesn't have issues. When you have asked your partner several times and your requests have been ignored, a conversation needs to happen.

A lot of the learning involved in being able to confront your partner is actually your own self-work. Human beings tend to avoid confrontation. We have a fear of tempers rising and relationships ending. But to be truly happy in a relationship, you have to be able to hold that line between when to let things go and when to break some eggs.

When an issue is continually being ignored, I teach the ABC approach to communication. When confronting your partner on an issue, state:

A – The **ACT** (or behavior) you keep seeing in your partner

B – The **BASE** message your partner seems to be communicating through that behavior

C – The **CONSEQUENCE** of what will happen if that behavior continues

A typical couple conversation often goes like this:

Honey, I'd like you to spend more time with me on the weekends.

Okay, that sounds good. We'll do it next weekend.

You said that last weekend and the weekend before, but nothing changed.

Why are you always so needy? I need to spend time with my friends on the weekend, too.

(Conversation ends. Frustration and resentment begin.)

The ABC Approach to Communication goes like this:

Honey, I'd like you to spend more time with me on the weekends.

Sure, that sounds good.

You said that last time and didn't make a change. **(ACT)**

Yeah, I know, but I need to spend time with my friends. You are so needy.

Listen, if you don't want to spend time with me anymore, let me know, because it makes me think you're not happy in this relationship. **(BASE MESSAGE)**

What? Yeah, I'm into it. Sorry.

Well, to be honest, I'm not seeing it, and we've had this conversation a number of times. I don't feel like I'm an important part of your life. If you don't want to be with me, that's fine, but maybe we should end things now. We will eventually break up if this doesn't change anyway. **(CONSEQUENCE)**

Conversations between partners are often nuanced, and the messages are hidden. This is what creates the problem. The beauty of the ABC approach to communication is that it removes all internal dialogue and puts everything right there on the table to be discussed.

Now, this is a powerful approach. Do not use it for issues like what you should watch on Netflix. It also isn't needed when you are with someone who understands there is a problem but just doesn't know how to fix it; then you just come see me. Use the ABC method when there is a significant problem that needs to be discussed and your partner just keeps ignoring you.

The key when having this conversation is to stay calm and neutral. Use language like: "If you don't want to spend time with me, just let me know so I can make a decision about what to do next."

Notice how different that language is from: "I can't believe you don't want to be with me!" The calmer you are, the less you will be pulled in that unconscious relationship dynamic that occurs when tempers get high.

This approach works especially well with people who lack personal insight. Women in general tend to act more from a place of personal insight in a relationship, and men act in reaction to something that has happened.

A woman's inner dialogue might be: *He's not treating me very well. If things don't change, I'm going to need to leave him.*

A man's inner dialogue might be: *She hasn't left yet, so things can't be too bad.*

I'd say 95 percent of women I do counseling with see me before the relationship has ended. And 95 percent of men call me in a panic over the phone, saying:

"My wife just walked out. I don't know what happened."

"Did she say there were problems in the relationship?"

"Yes, she's been telling me for years, but I didn't take them seriously."

"Okay, well, you probably should have."

Once a woman has made a decision to leave, it is very difficult to get her back (I'm stereotyping here). She has passed what I call the *threshold of hope.* She has given up on the idea that the relationship can improve and she can be happy.

Though I find my statements on the difference between how men and women might think quite funny, I often find them to also be true. The more insight a man has (or the less a woman has), the less this is the case.

The ABC approach to communication bridges these two ways of thinking, linking personal insight to consequences. One caveat is that you have to be willing to walk away (or do something else extreme) if you do not get your needs met; otherwise, you are communicating to your partner that it's not a big deal if he or she continues to dismiss you. In other words, there is no consequence.

4. Boundaries

While being able to ask for what you want in a relationship is key, it is also imperative that you become skilled at setting boundaries with your partner. Setting boundaries can help make things clear when issues arise. And setting boundaries is not simply about saying, "I have to go out with my friends tonight" or "You can't talk to me like that"—it's about having your own unique identity that you bring to and maintain throughout the relationship. Often as we become romantically involved with someone, we can't help but get lost in the dreaminess of our partner. We want to spend all our time with him or her, and we let go of our sense of who we are. We stay in bed with our partner all the time, are late for work, or ignore family and friends for the first couple of weeks. In extreme cases, we start wearing the same Christmas sweaters to the staff Xmas party.

Once the honeymoon period ends, however, you need to get back your own personal identity. Keeping a part of yourself separate from your partner and your passions alive is not only healthy but also helps maintain attraction long-term. By maintaining separateness from your partner, you appreciate the person as a whole, unique individual who is different from you. He or she has different interests and beliefs. That separateness creates desire, as we always want what we don't have and want to pull it closer to us. Add in love and understanding, and you have a great mix for a happy relationship.

5. Remember, It's Always Up to You

To be happy and get what you want, you must go out and get it. We can sometimes be a bit lazy, thinking that someone else is supposed to bring us all our happiness on a silver platter. However, life doesn't work that way. You have to make it happen.

But don't think too much. I often find that I'll have a conversation with myself on how I think I should behave with a partner but have never actually asked her if that's what she wants. Only later do I discover she wanted me to do the exact opposite of what I was doing!

Open up and take chances. You'll soon discover there are an infinite number of new opportunities available to you, if you only ask.

Visit www.TheRelationshipCode.com to access all your bonus material, including your *free* online course.

CHAPTER 8

Why Chopsticks Make Bad Girlfriends

Strategy #8
Avoid Dating Overly Rigid People

1. Rigid people view the world in a very static way.

2. A person who is rigid is very threatened by change.

3. The deeper any relationship gets, the more someone is asked to change.

4. A rigid person will choose his or her current reality over a new reality with you.

I recently sat across the table from an attractive woman at a speed-dating event. During speed dating, you have six minutes to discover if you are compatible with someone.

She initiated the conversation briskly.

"What do you do?" she asked without sentiment.

It was a job interview.

"Hang on a moment," I said, "Let's just relax."

I get mixed results when I tell someone I'm a psychologist right away. Half the people find it interesting, and the other half think I'm analyzing them.

I attempted to slow down the tempo of the conversation instead. "Let's start with you," I said with a smile. "What do you do for a living?"

"I'm a nurse. And you?"

Right back at me. Already I knew we probably weren't compatible.

I felt the impulse to soften my conversation style, but I resisted, as I didn't want to fill in the opposite energy in this relationship already.

"Tell me more about what it's like being a nurse first."

She had a sharpness and an efficient way of interacting with me that lasted the entire six minutes.

I checked her off as a possibility on my dating card anyway because she was attractive. Guys do that.

After the speed-dating event, I had the opportunity to talk to her again.

She had had a difficult childhood and wasn't very trusting of people. Unfortunately, this had led to her attracting poor-quality men in her life.

An hour into our conversation, I was making good headway. We were connecting at an emotional level, and I was starting to like her.

"I have two rules that I never break when I date a

man," she stated out of nowhere. "The first is, I never date a man who rides a motorcycle. I don't even consider those people."

I had just bought a motorcycle.

We never got to the second rule.

We have a tendency to think everyone will change, that they will adapt when an opportunity arises for greater happiness. Often people will not.

Change is hard, as we prefer to stick with what we know instead of what we don't. The mind prefers things to stay the same. It makes life feel safe and predictable.

Ironically, though, we are trying to continually keep our life the same while at the same time wanting it to change for the better.

People with rigid beliefs have extreme difficulty with this. The reason is they don't have a deep sense of who they are, which creates insecurity. Instead, they define themselves or the world by rigid, overly generalized beliefs such as: "I'm a hard nut to crack," "All men are like this," or "Everyone will try to take advantage of you at some point." They then live in this rigid reality, which is difficult to change.

Being in a relationship with someone like this is risky because you will undoubtedly challenge their reality as you try to blend your life with theirs. They will feel very threatened.

Don't Be Too Rigid Yourself

"It is not the strongest of the species that survives but the most adaptable." —Charles Darwin

We all have a tendency to be rigid in some ways, but an adaptable person is able to adjust to new circumstances much more quickly.

Let's say I order a pizza and I'm an adaptable person, and the pizza turns up cold. I might say, "Oh, that's too bad, but I'll just microwave it." I still might be upset, but I'll adjust to the situation. The pizza is cold. What can you do? I go with the reality of the situation and make the best of it.

However, if I'm an overly rigid person, I'll do the opposite. I'll try to adjust the external circumstances to match my inner expectations. I'll say, "This pizza is supposed to be hot. This is terrible customer service. I'm going to file a complaint with your manager."

The adaptable person sees the reality and adjusts to it. The rigid person tries to control the reality by imposing his or her beliefs more strongly upon it.

Now, there is a balance here. You do not want to be so soft and wishy-washy that you don't get your needs met. We all need to have a certain degree of rigidity to our beliefs, but you don't want to be so controlling that you are imposing your views on everyone else all the time. This will create a lot of unnecessary unhappiness within you.

A Rigid Person vs. an Abusive Person

Everyone has been in a controlling relationship to some degree (or been controlling themselves). Oftentimes we are just trying to figure things out. We have already discussed how rigid people can end a relationship early because they find it threatening and how that can lead to heartbreak.

In more extreme cases, abuse can occur. True abuse is when someone displays a chronic pattern of trying to force another person into their reality. They do this by trying to break down the other person's beliefs, emotions, and self-esteem to fit better with the reality they have in their mind. These people aren't fun to be with and can also be violent and unpredictable, so you should avoid them at all costs. You can avoid them by being very aware of your opposite relationship dynamic, being open and authentic, and ensuring that you are always being treated well.

An escape from an abusive relationship can occur when your true self is ignited and you no longer care about the reality you are trying to maintain with this person. Then freedom is possible.

How Being Overly Defensive Attracts Jerks

I want to go back to the speed-dating example at the start of this chapter to finish up. This woman had a very rigid belief system, and it was unfortunately holding her back from meeting high-quality men. She had been deeply hurt in the past, which had caused her to set up walls around herself. Now, it is a natural response to want set up walls around yourself after getting hurt, but paradoxically it can make things worse.

We hold this Rapunzel-like belief that the right person will climb our defenses and take us away. But this thinking is fundamentally flawed. If you have high defenses, nice men with integrity won't climb those walls. They will respect you. Only the jerks will climb those walls because they don't respect you.

Women unknowingly filter out many good men by expecting them to climb those high fences. This is how women can attract stalkers as well as married men who cheat on their wives. If you create an extreme environment with thorns and a large moat, only extreme people will cross it (and not the good extreme type). And you will let them in because everyone seeks love and attention at their core.

So instead of defensiveness, seek to experience life and try new things. Be open and genuine. And if you have defenses up (as we all do), remove them brick by brick. It's the best way to attract high-quality people in your life and avoid the ones who aren't worth your effort.

Visit www.TheRelationshipCode.com to access all your bonus material, including your *free* online course.

CHAPTER 9

Accepting Yourself

Strategy #9
Accept Who You Are

I tell my friends that resistance is going against how your life is naturally unfolding and then beating yourself up about it. All our beliefs, fears, and defense mechanisms prevent us from following the simplest path to happiness. We think we know what we are doing sometimes when we don't. But if we could just stop controlling how we "think" things should be and could drop our assumptions, life would flow much more naturally.

Excessive Thinking Is Not Valuable

To have a naturally effortless life, we must do several things, and the first is to drop excess mental chatter.

In all aspects of life, especially relationships, excess thinking gets in the way of finding a sense of peace and happiness.

When left to its own devices, our mind creates many

useless thoughts and poor judgments about ourself and other people. Most of them are random and untrue, and are just a way to maintain our own status quo.

Excessive thinking is not valuable. Insight is valuable. Creative expression is valuable. Reasoned discussion is valuable. Worrying too much isn't.

Worrying also short-circuits creativity and new ideas. This is why meditation and finding other ways to calm down are beneficial. When you can experience more calmness in your mind and within your life, you see things more clearly and can deal with them more effectively.

You've probably had the experience of being late for work and not being able to find your keys. You start digging through drawers and rushing around. Then maybe you take a breath and calm down—and you remember exactly where you put them.

The more peaceful and calm you can be when you are in a relationship, the easier it will be. Getting excited, screaming, and reacting do little to get your needs met. Sometimes it can be necessary to get angry, but reactive (or unconscious) anger based on first suppressing your needs and then exploding at your partner is never useful. Conscious (or aware) anger can be used to indicate that a problem needs to be addressed. You then let go of the anger as soon as it is no longer needed.

When in doubt, take a break and meditate. Take five

or ten minutes to sit with your thoughts and breathe, or go out and take a long, slow walk. You'll then be able to see the big picture, which always lies at the depth of the emotional experience, not on the surface.

Interestingly, with all the clients I have worked with, their biggest realizations about what to do in a relationship have come from a place of calmness and distance. They achieve a sense of personal detachment from the circumstances around them. And that is often when they either decide to stay and work it out or realize it is over. When the mind is erratic, thoughts are choppy, as if you are caught in a storm, and it's difficult to know which way to go.

By practicing calmness and by taking some time for yourself—going for a walk in nature, relaxing, meditating, or exercising—the mind often calms. You come into your heart and connect more with the truth of the situation, not just your superficial worries. This allows you to relax and find the effortlessness in life once again. And you can then talk to your partner, if applicable.

Another trick is to not look to find the perfect situation to start being happy. There is no perfect situation. There are only questions you need to ask about the situation: "Can I be happy now?" "Can I embrace opportunities for even more happiness in my life?" "Can I see happiness in my future?"

The Acceptance Exercise

Take out a piece of paper and a pencil, and draw a line down the center of the page. On the left side, write down all the things you don't like about yourself. Then on the right side, write down all the things you like about yourself.

You'll probably come up with more negatives than positives, but be bold with some of the great, wonderful things about you, too.

Don't think too much—just write as much as possible.

When you're done, review the negative and positive sides. Then erase the middle line or cover it up, and read everything on the page as one big thing. No longer categorize anything as good or bad. They are all the same.

Try to notice how some of your bad traits are really good traits if taken from a different perspective. So if you have a temper, appreciate how sometimes getting mad spurs others to action. If you are a sensitive person, become aware of how that characteristic allows you to be more deeply caring and sensitive to others' needs.

The point is not to judge good or bad, because what is good or bad? Notice how fluid judgments can be and how your "bad" aspects can also be beautiful when seen in a different light.

Notice how when you combine all your aspects, you

see a very colorful, wonderfully flawed person—a very unique individual.

You can also share your list with some trusted friends. You'll be surprised to find that they see some of your "bad" traits as some of your best traits and the reasons they like you so much. This is all a part of seeing who you are.

Accepting Yourself

There is a calmness that comes from accepting who you are without judgment. Your mind no longer races, and a peace resides within you. When you judge yourself harshly, you split yourself into two pieces—the judging part and the real you. Instead of peace, you create worry and self-doubt. You are no longer able to relax and just be yourself.

Instead, simply relax and accept yourself. Accept how you are right now and see how everything goes.

Let's say, for example, you are in a relationship and you want to have a serious conversation with your partner about why you are not getting your needs met. Maybe the conversation doesn't go well. That's okay because you're moving in the right direction. Accept what happened. Accept what you did and let everything else unfold naturally.

Patience and allowing things to happen often produce results we do not expect. Also, let the other person respond as he or she wishes. Give the other person the opportunity to have his or her own experience and learn from it, too.

When you don't accept what has happened (or beat yourself up about it), you stop change from happening at a higher level than your mind can perceive, and you cut yourself off from the deeper understanding that was about to arrive through patience and allowing things to unfold naturally. And if action is then needed, you take it.

> "Tension is who you think you should be.
> Relaxation is who you are."
> —Chinese proverb

By simply accepting and getting your thoughts and judgments out of the way, you allow yourself to move more deeply into your own place of wisdom and personal peace and toward the path of true happiness.

Returning to the Present

When you come from a place of calmness and acceptance, you can also more easily tune in to the present moment. Is there anything more satisfying than being in the now? You might say yes, but the answer is no. When you are here now, you are fully experiencing everything the world has to offer. You are lit up with all the sights, sounds, smells, tastes, and sensations of being human. There is an inherent feeling of life satisfaction that becomes available when you come into the Now.

One of the reasons we are often unhappy is that we are searching for something in the future (such as a new relationship or a new job) and miss the greatness of what is happening now. It is impossible to be truly satisfied if you cannot come in to the present moment because the present is the only place where your heart and body reside. Every time you think about the future, you come out of the present and your body, and the fullness of life diminishes. Allow yourself to be present now.

As you learn to let go of your thoughts and judgments, as you learn to relax and accept yourself more, you'll find that the present moment arrives much more easily. You'll understand yourself more and how to have all your needs and desires met in an effortless way.

"What you seek is seeking you."   —Rumi

Visit www.TheRelationshipCode.com to access all your bonus material, including your *free* online course.

CHAPTER 10

Life Is a Mirror

Spoiler Alert: It all works out.

Strategy #10
Relationships Are a Reflection of Where You Are At in Your Life

I've gotten to the point in my life where I've forgotten why I ever wanted be in a relationship. I no longer think that way. Previously, I thought I was missing something by not being in a relationship—that somehow the people on the other side were having much more fun. Some may be, but many are not. Being single or in a relationship are simply different paths. We will all experience both sometime in our lives.

But as my awareness of who I am and why I am on the planet grows, I now realize that we are always exactly where we need to be.

In fact, at a spiritual level, we are choosing exactly where we need to be in order to find our own happiness

—a happiness that is not dependent on another person.

I've been in many types of relationships—beautiful ones and crazy ones. I have found peace within relationships, and I have found peace without them. It's always about deepening and creating yourself first because you are the most important thing on the planet for you.

Where you are at is exactly where you need to be at a deep level. If you stop judging yourself about where you think you should be, you will be pleasantly surprised at where you are at right now in your life and what you are looking to learn. Consider how powerful your current situation is instead of viewing it from a place of lack.

I once had a conversation with a dear friend who said, "How can I find someone who makes me happy when I'm not happy myself?"

The answer is, you can't.

We like to think we can somehow upgrade our level of happiness by being with someone else, that we can just skip over our own personal awareness steps but no matter where you go, you are always taking yourself with you. You take your self-esteem and self-limiting beliefs wherever you go.

And as we have previously discussed, those beliefs create a reality in your head that you continue to repeat in your life until you become more aware and make changes. Without inner change, you end up with the same type of relationship over and over again.

How to Change Your Relationships

Use these five steps as guidance:

1) Move away from *Unconscious Relationships*. These types of relationships are based on childhood history and an unconscious way of making decisions. Almost everyone in a good or bad relationship who *ended up* with another person without being truly aware of how they did is in this stage. The underlying motivation for staying in an unconscious relationship is the avoidance of fear and the desire to feel comfortable and be safe.

This is also the stage where nasty breakups and expensive divorce litigations occur when things go awry.

2) Move into a *Mindful Relationship* with yourself. How can you change things if you don't know what you are consciously doing? In this stage, you start to become aware of your own needs, wants, and self-limiting thought patterns. You begin to self-nurture and ask to have your needs met by another. You may also begin to realize that you can have much more in a relationship than you have been previously attracting.

You don't necessarily know how to get exactly what you want, but you are aware that much more is possible than you are currently achieving.

3) Engage in a *Conscious Relationship* with someone else. This is a type of working relationship in which both people are helping each other learn, grow, and become better people.

I tell my couples, "Think of yourselves as students who are working together on a personal growth project at school." I recommend they try new approaches to connecting and communicating and give each other feedback. I have them practice what I call "deep communication," which is essentially speaking more from a place of emotional openness. I then ask them to do more of what works and less of what doesn't, which is essentially doing more of what makes the two of them feel better as a couple.

If things happen to end in this type of relationship, breakups (including divorces) are much more civil and are based on mutual understanding. There is a realization that the partners are simply not compatible with respect to their dreams, values, and personality types. They may still remain dear friends. There may still be tears at the end of this type of relationship, but there is less anger and resentment.

4) Move into an *Effortless Relationship* with yourself and then others. This is the type of relationship in which two people know who they are and what they are looking for in a partner to enjoy and appreciate life with

(they are not overly rigid in their vision, though). Difficult events still happen, but they are problems that are dealt with lovingly, with a desire for understanding and resolution. A difference of opinion becomes more about an appreciation of differences rather than a reason to belittle or attack one another. Both partners share the goal of finding a deeper truth that neither could see on his or her own.

5) The *Relationship of Change*. This is the fifth stage of relating with another. The two people work together at a very high level of synchronicity, helping others as they support each other's strengths and weaknesses. They also very much enjoy their time and life together. They help change the planet in their own way and have found a completeness within themselves.

The Relationship of Change is beyond the scope of this book but is something to think about and to look to attract if you're interested.

If you are in a higher relationship stage, be aware that you may drop down to a lower stage during a time of crisis or because you need to spend a little more time at a lower stage to learn more. Don't judge yourself. Simply relax, accept, and learn from it. Consider it an adventure. If action is necessary, take it. You will eventually move to a more peaceful stage once again.

If you are becoming increasingly frustrated with the types of relationships you attract, most likely it is because you are following an unconscious role (or set of rules) that no longer serves you.

To have the relationships you want, you have to live the life you want.

Drop your role (and rules) and embrace who you really are. Create your ideal life and leave your past behind.

Rebooting Your Relationships

If you limit yourself, you will have limited relationships—it's that simple. Your relationships are a reflection of you. When you change your beliefs and the way you are interacting with yourself, you change the type of relationships you will have with others. If you are in a relationship, you can also radically change your current relationship when you do this. And if your partner is open to receiving this new dynamic, you get the upgrade to Relationship 2.0.

And remember, people often think that if they simply change their situation (such as divorcing their partner or dating someone new), their life will radically change. Oftentimes it won't, because you can't escape yourself.

To attract better relationships and leave poorer ones, you need to understand your needs, your values, and your desires, and then begin to request those things from yourself and others.

It's not always an easy process. In the end, the goal is to be happy with yourself, and with someone else as the opportunity arises.

But there can never be a definitive map to the perfect relationship. You can have guidelines, but you must also learn to stray from them. When it comes to the heart, you must always be open to what you have never before experienced. There are things to explore that you have never considered would bring you happiness. The trick is to be able to see the good opportunities and skip the bad ones. If you learn, grow and become more yourself throughout the entire process, you'll do just fine.

How To Get Started

Often when I do relationship counseling with single women, they wonder why they're not meeting anyone.

They want to meet someone new, but they don't want to do anything new.

If you continue to go to the same Starbucks every day and talk to the same coworkers every day, nothing surprising is going to happen in your life. You must step out of your old reality. You must go out and try new things. But more importantly, you have to be open, powerful, and vulnerable, regardless of past hurts, in order to allow change to occur within yourself.

No one is going to knock on your door and ask you out. You have to step into a new reality to meet new people. This doesn't mean you just randomly go out and do stuff you don't like. You have to use your insight to say, "Hey, I'm open to trying this, even though I'm a little scared."

Perhaps you need to go for counseling to receive additional help. If so, just call or email me and we can do some work together.

If you are interested in one of my group coaching programs or attending one of my fun three-day retreats, you can get more information on my website at: www.The RelationshipCode.com.

Finally, if you meet someone new, have no agenda and instead simply see how things naturally unfold. Learn and grow through the experience. Eventually the way you interact with yourself will become more effortless, and you will be able to attract relationships more effortlessly.

Final Thoughts

Relationships—so fun, so confusing, so joyful. They can be both heartbreaking and life changing, but we press on. Why? Because they are the very fabric of how we interact on this planet. We have relationships with ourselves, others, and the planet around us. Like it or not, relationships are the essence of what makes us human, and they are here to stay.

Final Tips

1. You'll know more tomorrow than you know today. So don't be too hard on yourself if you make a mistake. Let it go and move on—you are always learning, growing, and becoming a better person. Be nicer to yourself than you think you should.

2. Start all relationships with an open heart. End all relationships with a closed mind.

To experience anything new, you have to be open to it—you have to be willing to open your heart. But when you find you are not getting your needs met and it looks as though that is not going to change, you need to close that relationship down with your mind.

Unfortunately, the heart loves to remain open, even when we're in a bad situation. That's why you need to be able to use your mind to exit the situation.

3. Be loving and kind in general. One of the sad things I have begun to see recently is that we don't particularly value kindness so much anymore. It's not flashy or interesting enough, I guess. No one's going to buy movie tickets or watch a reality show if there's not a

lot of trouble happening. But in a relationship, kindness is so sweet. Let's bring kindness back into the picture. Kindness is never out of fashion. In fact, it's sexy.

4. Finally, it's not about getting it right. It's about knowing and being true to yourself and seeing where the world takes you. Let go of your beliefs about needing to be in a relationship (or not). Let go of your judgments about whether you are successful or a failure if you're not in a relationship. Just relax. Let the world and your awareness take you where you wish to go. Wisdom flows downstream, and if you are aware and open, you always end up happy.

Visit www.TheRelationshipCode.com to access all your bonus material, including your *free* online course.

Afterword

I hope you enjoyed this book. I've put my heart, soul, and sixteen years of counseling into it to help you make better relationship choices. Hopefully, I will help you avoid some of the potholes and find more joy along the way.

In this book, I've given you many ideas on how not to get caught up in the psychological traps and ways of thinking that get people stuck in bad relationships. By gaining a better understanding of yourself and your relationships, you are choosing to attract better ones.

And while understanding the mind can be a valuable tool to increase awareness around the choices you are making, that is not the end goal. The goal is to move toward living life more intuitively from a place of appreciation, love, and awareness where you are not limited by your preexisting beliefs and patterns. That's how you attract truly healthy relationships as well, by being a flower opening to the sun.

That's the journey, whether you are in a relationship or not.

Wishing you much love and success on all your travels.
—Heron Free

Acknowledgments

I'd like to thank everyone who supported me on this journey—friends, family, clients, and random strangers who unwittingly gave me ideas. I'd also like to thank everyone who was excited about my book before it was completed. They inspired me to keep going and helped me realize I was onto something. I'd also like to thank my editor, Kira Freed, who was amazing with respect to my late-night emails and book edits.

I'd especially like to thank my mom, who supported her son in wanting to change the world in his own unique way, and for supporting my completely unrealistic way of doing things. Moms are like that. I love you and couldn't have done it without you.

As always, life is a group project.

This book took me ten years to write.

"To thine own self be true."

About the Author

Heron Free, M.Ed., RPsych., is a master psychologist and relationship expert. He has been in private practice for over sixteen years. He has helped thousands of people better understand themselves, relationships, and life.

Find out more at amazon.com/author/heronfree

Or visit www.TheRelationshipCode.com
    www.heronfree.com

52673605R00068

Made in the USA
Charleston, SC
24 February 2016